FACEBOOK MARKETING WORKBOOK:
HOW TO USE FACEBOOK
FOR BUSINESS

2016 EDITION

BY JASON MCDONALD, PH.D.

© 2015-2016, JM INTERNET GROUP

https://www.jm-seo.org/

Tel. 800-298-4065

INTRODUCTION

Welcome to the *Facebook Marketing Workbook, 2016 edition*! Get ready to

- have some **fun**;
- **learn how Facebook works;**
- understand how to use **Facebook** to **market your business**; and
- create a step-by-step **Facebook marketing plan**.

Fully revised and updated for 2016, this workbook not only explains how to market on Facebook but also provides access to **free** Facebook marketing tools. It provides overviews, step-by-step instructions, tips and secrets, free tools for Facebook marketing, and (*wait, there's more!*) access to worksheets that will help you build a systematic Facebook marketing plan. Even better, if you register your copy, you also get access to my complete *Social Media Toolbook*, with literally hundreds of free social media marketing tools to turbocharge your social media marketing not just on Facebook but also on LinkedIn, Twitter, YouTube, Google+, Instagram and other major social media platforms.

> *It slices, it dices. It explains how to Facebook works. It gives you free tools. And it helps you make a Facebook marketing plan.*

If you're really gung-ho for **social media marketing**, I refer you to my *Social Media Workbook*, an all-in-one guide to the entire social media universe from Facebook to LinkedIn, Twitter to YouTube, Instagram to Pinterest, Yelp to Google+, and everything in between. Learn more about that book at http://jmlinks.com/social or call 800-298-4065.

Why Market via Facebook?

If you've read this far, you're definitely intrigued by Facebook as a marketing platform. Perhaps you're just starting out with a **Facebook Page** for your **business**. Or perhaps you already have a Page, but want to make it really work. Let's step back for a minute and ask: **why market on Facebook**?

Here are some reasons:

- **Facebook is big.** Facebook is the largest social media platform, with over one billion users worldwide and climbing.
- **Facebook is ubiquitous.** Nearly everyone uses Facebook – from teenagers to grandmas, business executives to flight attendants. Facebook – as we shall see – is all about friends, family, fun, and photos. By participating in Facebook, you can reach your customers where they "hang out."
- **Facebook is free**. Facebook is, of course, free to use. And in terms of marketing there is a lot you can do, for free, to build your brand, spread eWOM (electronic word of mouth), help you stay top-of-mind with your customers, and even "get shares" or "go viral."
- **Facebook has advertising.** If you advertise smart on Facebook, and combine paid advertising with free organic Facebook marketing, you can demographically target not only your current customers but also prospective customers, thereby radically extending the reach of your online marketing efforts.

Facebook, however, is also complicated. Using it is one thing, and marketing on Facebook is another. Most businesses fail at Facebook marketing because they just don't "get it." They don't understand how Facebook works, and they fail to see the incredible marketing opportunities beneath the surface of the Zuckerberg empire. Quite simply, you have to invest some time to learn "how" to market on Facebook.

Enter the *Facebook Marketing Workbook*.

Who is this Workbook For?

This workbook is aimed primarily at **small business owners** and **marketing managers**. Non-profits will also find it useful.

If you are a person whose job involves advertising, marketing, and/or branding, this workbook is for you. If you are a small business that sees a marketing opportunity in Facebook, this workbook is for you. And if your job is to market a business or organization online in today's Internet economy, this book is for you. Anyone who wants to look behind the curtain and understand the mechanics of how to market on Facebook will benefit from this book.

Anyone who sees – however dimly – that Facebook could help market their business will benefit from this hands-on guide.

How Does This Workbook Work?

This workbook starts first with an overview to **social media *marketing***. If social media is a **party**, then **using social media** is akin to just *showing up*. **Marketing** on social media, in contrast, isn't about showing up. It's about *throwing* the party!

Understanding that distinction between "attending" the social media party and "throwing" the social media party is the subject of **Chapter One.**

Chapter Two is a deep dive into Facebook marketing. We'll overview how Facebook works, explain everything from profiles to pages, likes to comments to shares, Edgerank to posting rhythm. It will all become much clearer, as we work through Facebook in plain English, written for "mere mortals." Along the way, I'll provide **worksheets** that will act as "Jason as therapist," so you can fill them out and begin to outline your own unique Facebook marketing plan.

Finally, this workbook ends with an **Appendix**: a list of amazing **free Facebook tools** and resources. Even better, if you register your copy, you get clickable online access to the tools, a PDF copy of the book, and (wait, there's more!) a complimentary copy of my *Social Media Toolbook*, my compilation of hundreds of social media tools not just for Facebook but for all the major platforms.

Here's how to register your copy of this workbook:

1. Go to https://jm-seo.org/workbooks
2. Click on Facebook.
3. Use this password: **facebook2016**
4. You're in. Simply click on the link for a PDF copy of the *Social Media Toolbook* as well as access to the worksheets referenced herein.

OK, now that we know what this workbook is about, who it is for, and our plan of action...

Let's get started!

≫ MEET THE AUTHOR

My name is Jason McDonald, and I have been active on the Internet since 1994 (having invented the Internet along with Al Gore) and taught SEO, AdWords, and Social Media since 2009 – online, at Stanford University Continuing Studies, at both AcademyX and the Bay Area Video Coalition in San Francisco, at workshops, and in corporate trainings across these United States. I love figuring out how things work, and I love teaching others! Social media marketing is an endeavor that I understand, and I want to empower you to understand it as well.

Learn more about me at https://www.jasonmcdonald.org/ or at my corporate website https://www.jm-seo.org/. Or just call 800-298-4065, say something flattering, and I my secretary will put you through. *(Like I have a secretary! Just call if you have something to ask or say).*

≫ SPREAD THE WORD: WRITE A REVIEW & GET A FREE eBOOK!

If you like this workbook, please take a moment to write an honest review on Amazon.com. *If you hate the book, feel free to trash it on Amazon or anywhere across the Internet. (I have thick skin). If you hate life, in general, and are just one of those bitter people who write bitter reviews… well, gosh, go off and meditate, talk to a priest or do something spiritual. Life is just too short to be that bitter!*

At any rate, here is my special offer for those lively enough to write a review of the book–

1. Write your **honest review** on Amazon.com.
2. **Contact** me via https://www.jm-seo.org/contact and let me know your review is up.
3. Include your **email address** and **website URL**, and any quick questions you have about it.
4. I will send you a **free** copy of one of my other eBooks which cover AdWords, SEO, and Social Media Marketing.

This offer is limited to the first 100 reviewers, and only for reviewers who have purchased a paid copy of the book. You may be required to show proof of purchase and the birth certificate of your first born child, cat, or goldfish. If you don't have a child, cat, or goldfish, you may be required to prove telepathically that you bought the book.

▶ QUESTIONS AND MORE INFORMATION

I **encourage** my students to ask questions! If you have questions, submit them via https://www.jm-seo.org/contact/. There are two sorts of questions: ones that I know instantly, for which I'll zip you an email answer right away, and ones I do not know instantly, in which case I will investigate and we'll figure out the answer together.

As a teacher, I learn most from my students. So please don't be shy!

▶ COPYRIGHT AND DISCLAIMER

Uh! Legal stuff! Get ready for some fun:

The information used in this guide was derived in July, 2015. However, social media marketing changes rapidly, so please be aware that scenarios, facts, and conclusions are subject to change without notice.

Additional Disclaimer. Internet marketing is an art, and not a science. Any changes to your Internet marketing strategy, including SEO, Social Media Marketing, and AdWords, is at your own risk. Neither Jason McDonald, Excerpti Communications, Inc., nor the JM Internet Group assumes any responsibility for the effect of any changes you may, or may not, make to your website or AdWords advertising based on the information in this guide.

» ACKNOWLEDGEMENTS

No man is an island. I would like to thank my beloved wife, Noelle Decambra, for helping me hand-in-hand as the world's best moderator for our online classes, and as my personal cheerleader in the book industry. Gloria McNabb has done her usual tireless job as first assistant, including updating this edition as well the *Social Media Marketing* toolbook. Alex Facklis and Hannah McDonald also assisted with tools and research. I would also like to thank my black Labrador retriever, Buddy, for countless walks and games of fetch, during which I refined my ideas about marketing and about life.

And, again, a huge thank you to my students – online, in San Francisco, and at Stanford Continuing Studies. You challenge me, you inspire me, and you motivate me!

PARTY ON

Most books on **social media marketing** (or **SMM** for short) either focus on the high, high level of hype, hype, hype or focus on the low, low, low level of micro technical details. It's either Malcolm Gladwell's *Blink*, Seth Godin's *Purple Cow*, David Meerman Scott's *The New Rules of Marketing and PR* – or it's *Social Media for Dummies*, *LinkedIn for Dummies*, or *Teach Yourself Facebook in Ten Minutes*.

You're either up in the sky, or lost in the weeds.

This book is different: it focuses on the middle, productive ground – part **theory**, and part **practice**. It gives you a framework for how to "think" about social media marketing as well as concrete advice on how to "do" social media marketing on Facebook in particular.

Throughout, it provides worksheets, videos, Todos and deliverables, to help you create a step-by-step social media marketing plan as well as a step-by-step Facebook plan. Used in combination with the *Social Media Toolbook*, which identifies hundreds of **free** tools for social media marketing all in one convenient place, small business owners and marketers finally have a practical, hands-on method for practical social media marketing.

This first chapter is about *how to think about social media marketing*. What is social media marketing? Why are you doing it? What should you do, step-by-step, to succeed?

Let's get started!

TO DO LIST:

>> Understand that Social Media Marketing is Like Throwing a Party

» Recognize the Social Media Marketing Illusion

» Identify Relevant Discovery Paths

» Establish Goals and KPIs

» Remember the Big Picture

» Deliverable: a "Big Picture" Social Media Marketing Plan

» UNDERSTAND THAT SOCIAL MEDIA MARKETING IS LIKE THROWING A PARTY

Have you ever **attended** a party? You know, received an invitation, showed up, said hello and various meets and greets to other guests, ate the *yummy yummy* food, drank the liquor (or the diet soda), hobnobbed with other guests, ate some more food, danced the night away, thanked the hosts, and left?

> *Attending* a party is all about *showing up*, *enjoying* the entertainment and food, and *leaving*.

Have you ever **used** Twitter? Facebook? Instagram? You know, logged in, checked out some funny accounts, read some posts, posted back and forth with friends and family, checked your updates, and then logged out?

That's *attending* a party. That's *using* social media.

> *Using* social media is all about *logging in*, *enjoying* what's new and exciting, and *logging out*.

Throwing a party, however, is something entirely different from **attending** a party. Similarly, **marketing** via social media is something entirely different from **using** social media.

This chapter explores the basics of social media *marketing*: of **throwing** the "social media party" vs. just **showing up**. That word *marketing* is very important: we're exploring how to use social media to enhance our brand, grow the visibility of our company, product or service, or even (gasp!) use social media to sell more stuff.

PARTY ON: BECOME A

GREAT PARTY-THROWER

Social media marketing is the art and science of throwing "great parties" on Facebook, LinkedIn, Pinterest and the like in such a way that people not only show up to enjoy the party but also are primed to buy your product or service.

Let's explore this analogy further: how is social media *marketing* like *throwing a party*?

Here are three ways:

Invitations. A great party needs great guests, and the first step to getting guests is to identify an attendee list, and send out invitations. Who will be invited? How will we invite them – will it be by phone call, email, postal mail, etc.? For your social media marketing, you'll need to identify your target audience(s) and brainstorm how to get them to "show up" on your social media page via tactics like sending out emails, cross-posting your Facebook to your Twitter, or your LinkedIn to your blog, advertising, or even using "real world" face-to-face invitations like "Hey, follow us on Twitter to get coupons and insider deals."

Social media marketing requires having a promotion strategy.

Entertainment. Will your party have a band, a magician, a comedian, or just music? What is your entertainment strategy? What kind of food will you serve: Mexican, Chinese, Tapas, or something else? Similarly for your social media marketing: why will people "hang out" on your Facebook page or YouTube channel? Will it be to learn something? Will it be because it's fun or funny?

Social media marketing requires having a content marketing strategy, a way to systematically produce yummy yummy content (blog posts, infographics, images, videos) that people will enjoy enough to "hang out" on your social media page or channel.

Hosting. As the host of your party, you'll "hang out" at the party, but while the guests are busy enjoying themselves, you'll be busy, meeting and greeting, making sure everything is running smoothly, and doing other behind-the-scenes tasks. Similarly, in your social media marketing, you'll be busy coordinating content, interacting with guests and even policing the party to "kick out" rude or obnoxious guests.

Social media marketing requires behind-the-scenes management, often on a day-to-day basis, to ensure that everything is running smoothly up to and including dealing with "rude" guests.

SOCIAL MEDIA MARKETING IS THROWING A PARTY

Oh, and one more thing. Let's assume, for example, you're going to throw your wife an amazing 40th birthday party. Before that party, you'll probably start attending other parties with a critical eye – noting what you like, and what you don't like, what you want to imitate, and even reaching out to the magicians, bands, and bartenders to find out what they cost and possibly hire them for your own party.

You'll "inventory" other parties and make a list of likes and dislikes, ideas and do-not-dos, and use that information to systematically plan your own party.

As a social media marketer, therefore, you should "attend" the parties of other brands online. Identify brands you like (REI, Whole Foods, Father Robert Barron), "follow" or "like" them, and keep a critical eye on what they're doing. **Inventory** your likes and dislikes, and **reverse engineer** what other marketers are up to. And in your industry, do the same: follow companies in your own industry, again with the goal of "reverse engineering" their social media marketing strategy, successes, and failures.

For your first TODO, identify some brands you admire and "follow" them on Twitter, LinkedIn, Facebook, Pinterest etc. Start making a list of what you like, or dislike, based on reverse engineering their online marketing strategy. Become a good user of social media, but with an eye to the marketing strategy "behind the scenes."

Successful social media is based on **illusion**, just like successful parties are based on illusion.

How so?

Let's think for a second about an amazing party. Think back to a holiday party you attended, a great birthday or graduation party, or even a corporate event. Was it fun? Did it seem magical? It probably did.

Now, if you've ever had the (mis)fortune of planning such an event – what was that like? Was it fun? Was it magical? Yes and no, but it was also probably a lot of work, "in the background," to make sure that the party ran smoothly.

Great parties have an element of **illusion** in them: they *seem* effortless, while *in reality* (behind the scenes) an incredible amount of strategy, planning, and hard work goes on. Similarly, great social media marketing efforts (*think Katy Perry or Lady Gaga on social media, think Whole Foods on social media, or REI, Zappos, Burt's Bees, or even Nutella*), create an illusion. They (only) "seem" spontaneous, they (only) "seem" effortless. But in the background a ton of work is going on to promote, manage, and grow these "social media parties."

ILLUSION IS COMMON TO GREAT PARTIES AND GREAT SOCIAL MEDIA MARKETING

With respect to social media marketing, this illusion often creates a weird problem for you vis-a-vis upper management or the boss. Upper management or your boss might mistakenly believe that "social media is easy," and/or "social media is free." You, as the marketer, might have to educate your boss that it only "looks" easy, or "seems" free. Social media marketing requires a ton of strategy, hard work, and (gasp!) even money or sweat equity to make it happen. Among your early tasks at social media marketing may be to explain the "social media marketing" illusion to your boss. It only seems easy. It only seems free.

For your second TODO, organize a meeting with your boss and/or marketing team. Discuss all the things that have to get done to be successful at social media marketing, ranging from conducting an **inventory** of competitor efforts, to **setting up basic**

accounts on Twitter, Facebook, LinkedIn, etc., to **creating content** to share on social media (images, photos, blog posts, infographics, videos), to **monitoring** social media channels on an on-going basis, and finally to **measuring** your successes. Educate the team that although it might not take a lot of money, social media marketing does take significant amount of work!

We're planning an awesome party here, people. It's going to take a ton of work, it's going to be a ton of fun, and it's going to be incredibly successful!

Now, don't get discouraged. *Please don't get discouraged.* As marketers, we are so fortunate to live in an amazing time with incredible new opportunities to reach our target customers.

- Is social media free? Yes (and no).
- Is it effortless? No.
- Is it worth it? Yes, yes, yes!

Social media marketing takes a lot of hard work, and it can be incredible. *Don't get discouraged!*

Know the Question and Find the Answer

Oh, and once you start to view social media marketing as a systematic process, a great thing will happen: you'll formulate concrete, specific questions. And, once you know a question you can find the answer.

Once you realize, for example, that Facebook allows cover photos, and that great Facebook marketers swap theirs out from time to time, you can create the "questions" of how do you create a cover photo for Facebook, what are the dimensions, etc.

IF YOU KNOW THE QUESTION, YOU CAN FIND THE ANSWER.

As you begin your social media marketing efforts, once you "know a question," simply go to Google to "find the answer." For example, simply Google "What are the dimensions of a Facebook cover photo" to end up on the Facebook help site or other websites that will tell you the answer. You now realize a) you need a series of compelling Facebook cover photos for your page, b) there are specific dimensions and policies required by Facebook, and c) either you or someone on your team has the "task" of making this happen on a regular basis.

>> IDENTIFY RELEVANT DISCOVERY PATHS

Before we plunge into Facebook, Twitter, and the gang, it's worthwhile to sit back and ponder the big questions of marketing. What do you sell? Who wants it and why? And, very directly: how do customers find you?

This last one might seem like a simple question, but a great social marketer has a very specific understanding of the paths by which customers find her product, service, or company. This understanding then guides -

> *How much should you focus on SEO (Search Engine Optimization)? How much should you focus on AdWords? How much on Facebook? Or Twitter? Should you buy ads on Television, or (gasp!) send out unsolicited email (spam)? Is Pinterest worth the effort?*

Once you brainstorm how customers find you, you will have a fundamental understanding of how to construct a systematic social media marketing plan.

Fortunately, there are only five paths of customer discovery. Only five. Every way that someone finds a product or service can be categorized by the following five **discovery paths**.

> **Search.** The search path occurs when the customer is "searching" for a company, product, or service. For example, a customer is hungry. He types into Google or Yelp, "pizza." He browses available restaurants, chooses one, and shows up to get pizza. *He searched for pizza. He found pizza. He made a decision.* The search path is the province of SEO (Search Engine Optimization), largely on Google but also on sites such as Yelp that work via "keywords" to help customers find stuff that they want.

Review / Recommend / Trust. The review / recommend /trust path is based on "trust indicators." In it, the customer already has created a list of vendors he or she might use, but he is researching "whom to trust." In this path, he might use the "reviews" and/or "stars" on Yelp or Google as "trust indicators" to predict which pizza restaurant is good (or bad). Reviews and stars are the most common trust indicators in social media marketing, but having a robust Facebook page, with many followers and interesting posts can also be a "trust indicator." Having an expert-looking profile on LinkedIn can be a "trust indicator" for a CPA or an architect. A recommendation from a friend or colleague also plays into reviews and trust.

eWOM / Share / Viral. Wow! That pizza was great! Let me take a selfie of me chowing down on the pizza, and post it to Instagram. Look friends: it's me, chowing down on pizza, having fun, livin' the life, while you're back in the dorm studying. Or, hey, Facebook friends, do you know of a great place to host a kid's birthday party? You do (electronic word of mouth). Or, wow, here is a cat video of cats at the pizza restaurant puzzled by the self-serve soda fountain. It's "gone viral" on YouTube and has sixteen million views! The share path occurs when a customer loves the product, service, or experience enough to "share" it on social media – be that via electronic word of mouth, a share on his or her Facebook page, a "selfie" on Instagram, or a viral video on YouTube.

Interrupt. The interrupt path is the bad boy of online marketing. Interrupt marketing occurs when you want to watch a YouTube video but before you can watch it *five, four, three, two, one,* you have to view an annoying ad. Or, when you get a spam email on "amazing Viagra." Interrupt is largely used in advertising, and largely used to "push" products that people aren't proactively looking for.

Browse. The browse path is a little similar to the interrupt path. In it, you're looking for something, reading something, or watching something, and alongside comes something else. For example, you go to YouTube to look up "how to tie a tie," and in the suggested videos at the end is a video for Dollar Shave Club. Or you see Dollar Shave Club videos suggested at the right of the screen. You're not proactively looking for Dollar Shave Club, but you see their information as you "browse" for related content on sites like YouTube, Facebook, or blogs.

First and foremost, social media marketing excels at the **share** path. Getting customers to share your product or service is, in many ways, the Holy Grail of social media marketing. But the Search path, the eWOM / Trust / Recommend path, and the Browse path are all also important.

For your third TODO, download the **Big Picture Marketing worksheet**. For the worksheet, go to https://www.jm-seo.org/workbooks (click on Facebook, enter the code 'facebook2016' to register if you have not already done so), and click on the link to the "Big Picture Marketing."

In this worksheet, you'll write a "business value proposition" explaining what you sell, and who are the target customers. You'll also identify the most relevant "discovery paths" by which potential customers find your products. That in turn, will get you to start thinking about which media are the most relevant to your online marketing efforts.

>> ESTABLISH GOALS AND KPIs (KEY PERFORMANCE INDICATORS)

Marketing is about measurement. Are we helping our brand image? Are we encouraging sales? How do we know where we are succeeding, and where there is more work to be done? Why are we spending all this blood, sweat, and tears on social media marketing anyway?

In today's overhyped social media environment, many marketers feel like they "must" be on Twitter, or they "must" have a presence on Pinterest. All of the social media companies – Facebook, Twitter, Pinterest, Yelp – have a vested interest in overhyping the importance of their platform, and using fear to compel marketers to "not miss out" by massively jumping on the latest and greatest social platform. Social media guilt, however, is to be avoided: if you define a clear business value proposition, know where your customers are, and establish clear goals and KPIs (Key Performance Indicators), you'll be able to focus on those social platforms that really help you and ignore the ones that are just hype.

AVOID SOCIAL MEDIA GUILT: YOU CAN'T (AND SHOULDN'T) DO EVERYTHING

Let's identify some common goals for effective social media marketing. The boss might have an ultimate "hard" goal of getting sales leads or selling stuff online. Those are definitely important, but as marketers, we might look to intermediary or "soft goals" such as nurturing a positive brand image online or growing our online reviews.

Generally speaking, social media excels at the "soft goals" of growing brand awareness, nurturing customer conversations, encouraging reviews and the like and is not so good at immediate, direct goals like lead captures or sales.

In any case, having high-level yet soft goals is essential to being able to create a systematic, social media marketing strategy as well as a "drilldown" strategy for an individual social medium, whether that be Twitter or LinkedIn, Instagram or YouTube.

Here are common goals for social media marketing:

eWOM (electronic Word of Mouth). Every brand wants people to talk about it in a positive way, and today a lot of that conversation occurs on social media. If we're a local pizza restaurant, we want people "talking" about us on Yelp, on Facebook, on Twitter as a great place to get pizza, eat Italian food, cater a wedding, or host a birthday party for little Jimmy. As marketers, a common goal for social media is to grow and nurture positive eWOM, which might be positive conversations on Facebook, positive reviews on Yelp or Google+ local, relationships between us and customers and among customers, and the sharing of our brand across media.

Customer Continuum. *A prospect becomes a customer, a customer becomes a fan, and a fan becomes an evangelist.* For example, I'm hungry. I search for "great pizza" in Palo Alto, California, and I find your pizza restaurant. I try your pizza, thereby becoming a customer. It's good, and I'm a fan: if someone asks me, I'll recommend Jason's Palo Alto Pizza. And finally, I love your pizza so much, I wrote a positive review on Yelp, I created a YouTube video of me eating your pizza, and I have a new blog on Tumblr about your pizza. As marketers, we want to encourage customers to move to the right on the customer continuum: from prospect to customer, customer to fan, and fan to evangelist. We are also aware of (and seek to mitigate) the "customer from hell" who can hate a brand so much that she writes a negative review on Yelp, posts negative comments on Facebook, or creates a viral YouTube about your terrible pizza (**reputation management**).

Trust Indicators. We want pizza. We look at reviews. We use reviews to decide which pizza restaurant is probably good. We want to go to a theme park. We look at their Facebook page. We choose the one that looks active, that looks like people are having fun. Trust indicators are all about mental "short cuts" that customers make to identify possible vendors, services, or products. A common goal of social media marketing, therefore, is to nurture positive trust indicators about our brand online: reviews, especially but not only.

One Touch to Many. You visit the pizza restaurant, one time. As a marketer, I want to convert that "one touch" to "many." I want you to follow us on Twitter, so I can Tweet special deals, promotions, what's cooking, and stay "top of mind," so that when you're hungry again, you think, Jason's Palo Alto Pizza. Using social media to convert one touch to many and stay top of mind is an excellent goal.

Promotion, promotion, promotion. Social sharing – getting customers to market your brand – is probably the most common social media goal. I want you to Instagram you and your kids having a great pizza party! I want you to share our amazing corporate catering event with your Facebook friends. Encouraging social sharing / eWOM / viral marketing is a huge, huge goal for SMM.

Social Media Marketing excels at the "soft goals" listed above. Note, in particular the desired "virtuous circle" of social media.

The more positive reviews I have on Yelp, the most customers I get, the most customers I get, the more positive reviews. The more followers on Twitter I get, the more chances I have to get them to share my discounts, the most discounts they share, the more followers I get. The more people like / share / comment on my Facebook page, the better my Edgerank (a measurement of how engaging one's content is), the better my Edgerank, the more people see my content, the more people see my content, the more shares I get on Facebook, the better my Edgerank.

NURTURE A VIRTUOUS CIRCLE

Nurturing a virtuous circle is a major, major goal of an effective social media marketing system. And finally, don't forget, that in most cases we want all of these "soft goals" to turn into "hard goals": a positive brand image to lead to more sales, and a stronger bottom line.

For your fourth TODO, download the **Marketing Goals Worksheet**. For the worksheet, go to https://www.jm-seo.org/workbooks (click on Facebook, enter the code 'facebook2016' to register if you have not already done so), and click on the link to the "Marketing Goals Marketing."

In this worksheet, you'll identify your "hard" goals, whether you have something "free" to offer, and your "soft" goals on social media. Ultimately, these big picture goals will be translated into much more specific goals, germane to a social medium such as YouTube, Twitter, or Facebook.

» ESTABLISH A CONTENT MARKETING SYSTEM

Bring on the chips! Carry out the diet coke! Turn on the band! A great party needs great food and great entertainment: these are the "fuel" of the successful party. Similarly, great social media marketing needs the "fuel" of content: interesting (funny, shocking, outrageous, sentimental) blog posts, images, photographs, infographics and instructographics, memes and even videos that will make it worthwhile to "subscribe" to your social channel (like / follow / circle) and keep coming back for more.

To succeed at social media marketing you must succeed at **content marketing**. You gotta gotta gotta create a system for identifying and creating interesting content to share via your social networks. Among the most commonly shared items are:

Images. Photographs and images are the bread-and-butter of Facebook, Instagram, and even Twitter.

Memes. From grumpy cat to success kid, memes make the funny and memorable, sticky and shareable on social media.

Infographics and Instructographics. From how to tie a tie to sixteen ways you can help stop global warming, people love to read and share pictures that tell a story, hopefully with facts.

Blog Posts. An oldie but goodie: an informative, witty, funny, informational, or fact-filled post about a topic that matters to your customers.

Slide Shows. From Slideshare to just posting your PowerPoints online, a hybrid visual and textual cornucopia of social sharing fun.

Videos. If a picture tells a thousand words, a video can tell ten thousand. YouTube is a social medium in its own right, but the videos themselves are content that can be enjoyed and shared.

In sum, you'll need fuel to power your social media marketing. This fuel comes in two main varieties: other people's content, and your own content. The advantage of the former is that it is easy to get, while the advantage of the latter is that because it's yours, you control the message. The disadvantage of other people's content is that you do not control the message (and it thereby promotes them to some extent), while the disadvantage of your own content is that its takes time and effort to produce.

To be an effective social sharer, you need both: **other people's content** and **your own content**.

Your goal is to position yourself (your company, your CEO, your brand) as a "useful expert," the "goto" person or brand that people come to to find interesting and useful stuff in your market ecosystem. My own brand, for example, at https://www.jasonmcdonald.org/ is all about sharing interesting, fun, and useful stuff on social media, AdWords, and SEO. That's why I have over 7,000 followers on Google+: because I'm useful.

Other People's Content

Fortunately, there are tools to help you systematically identify and share other people's content. (All are listed in the *Social Media Toolbook*, content marketing section). Here are some of my favorites:

Buzzsumo (http://buzzsumo.com) - Buzzsumo is a 'buzz' monitoring tool for social media. Input a website (domain) and/or a topic and see what people are sharing across Facebook, Twitter, Google+ and other social media. Great for link-building (because what people link to is what they share), and also for social media.

Topsy (http://topsy.com) - Real-time Twitter search engine. You can also search the web and videos. VERY important: you can input a URL, e.g., jm-seo.org or chipestimate.com, and see how frequently that URL and its sub URLs have been tweeted. Great way to see your social shares as well as discover what's trending on the blogosphere for more effective blogging.

Feedly (http://feedly.com) - Feedly is a newsreader integrated with Google+ or Facebook. It's useful for social media because you can follow important blogs or other content and share it with your followers. It can also spur great blog ideas.

Easely (http://easel.ly) - Use thousands of templates and design objects to easily create infographics for your blog. A competitor is Piktochart (http://piktochart.com).

Meme Generator (http://memegenerator.net) - Memes are shareable photos, usually with text. But how do you create them? Why, use memegenerator.net.

In terms of other people's content, you want to first identify the "themes" of social media about which you want to talk. An expert in tax issues, for example, might monitor California tax law, small business, and individual tax shelter issues. He can then systematically monitor them via a tool such as Feedly, and use Feedly to easily share other people's content across his social networks. A Palo Alto pizza restaurant might monitor content on the San Francisco Bay Area as well as pizza / italian food, and ideas for wedding catering and birthday parties. By being a "helpful sharer" of this information, the pizza restaurant can stay "top of mind" by providing useful content to people planning corporate events, weddings, and birthday parties as well as looking for fun things to do in the Bay Area.

Your Own Content

For your own content, the steps are to first brainstorm a useful content idea (e.g., an infographic on common ways for small business owners to save on taxes, or sixteen ways weddings can go terribly wrong), second to create it in whatever format you want (image, infographic, blog post, video), and third to share it across your relevant social networks. For managing your posts across social networks, I highly recommend Hootsuite (https://www.hootsuite.com/), which is a cloud-based social media management tool.

For your final TODO, download and complete the **Content Marketing Worksheet**. For the worksheet, go to https://www.jm-seo.org/workbooks (click on Facebook, enter the code 'facebook2016' to register if you have not already done so), and click on the link to the "Content Marketing Worksheet."

For a great list of the top ten tools for content marketing, please visit http://jmlinks.com/2h.

» REMEMBER THE BIG PICTURE

At this point, you've begun your social media marketing journey. You've understood that social media marketing is about "throwing" the party more than "attending the party." You've realized you need to start "paying attention" with regard to what other marketers are doing on social media, with an eye to "reverse engineering" their marketing strategy so that you have ideas of what you like, and do not like, in terms of social media. You've started to brainstorm "discovery paths" and "goals" for your SMM efforts.

And you've realized that once you've identified your goals, identified relevant social media, set up your social accounts, the really hard work will be a) promoting your social media channels, and b) creating the kind of content that makes them want to "like you," keep coming back for more, and share your message with their friends, family, and/or business colleagues.

You've understood that **promotion** and **content creation** are the big on-going tasks of successful social media marketing.

≫ DELIVERABLE: OUTLINE A SOCIAL MEDIA MARKETING PLAN

Now that we've come to the end of Chapter 1, your first DELIVERABLE has arrived. For the worksheet, go to https://www.jm-seo.org/workbooks (click on Facebook, enter the code 'facebook2016' to register if you have not already done so), and click on the link to the "Social Media Marketing Plan Big Picture Worksheet." By filling out this plan, you and your team will establish a vision of what you want to achieve via social media marketing.

Now it's time to drill into individual media, starting with the 800 lb. gorilla of social media, Facebook. Let's get started!

FACEBOOK

Facebook is a great place to begin your Social Media Marketing journey! Let me give you four good reasons.

First, Facebook is – by far – the largest social media platform, with over one billion active users and countless profiles, Pages, and groups. Nearly every person has a Facebook account ("profile"), many businesses have Pages, and survey after survey ranks Facebook as the most used social media platform. Second, once you understand the dynamics of Facebook – *Profiles and Pages, Timelines and Posts, Likes, Comments, and Shares...* you'll more easily understand other social media like Twitter or Instagram. Third, Facebook has a component in its algorithm called *Edgerank*, which is a measure of how interactive your business Page and posts are. Understanding what *Edgerank* is, and how to improve your *Edgerank* will help you be a better marketer on Facebook. It will also help with marketing on other social media sites, because all of them essentially calculate something like *Edgerank* in the background.

Finally, Facebook is fun! I think of Facebook as *friends, family, fun* and *fake*. (I'll explain *fake* in a moment.)

Let's get started!

To Do List:

» Explore how Facebook Works

» Inventory Companies on Facebook

>> Understand the Importance of Like & Edgerank

>> Set up and Optimize Your Page

>> Brainstorm and Execute a Posting Strategy

>> Promote Your Facebook Page and Posts

>> Measure your Results

>> Deliverable: a Facebook Marketing Plan

>> Appendix: Top Ten Facebook Marketing Tools and Resources

>> EXPLORE HOW FACEBOOK WORKS

To understand Facebook as a marketer is to understand the "F's": friends, family, fun, photos, and "fake." Before you set up (or optimize) a Facebook Page for your business, before you start posting, before you start advertising, and before you start measuring your successes and failures, take some time to research how Facebook works.

> *What are people doing on Facebook? Why do they like it? What are they sharing and interacting with? Are your customers on it, and if so, what are they doing? How might you interact with customers in a compelling, fun and non-obtrusive way?*

First, I'm assuming you have a personal Facebook profile; *if not, Mark Zuckerberg would like to talk with you.* Simply go to https://www.facebook.com/ and sign up. Facebook has a wonderful help section at https://www.facebook.com/help/ - just click on "get started on Facebook." Once you sign up – as an individual – you'll have a **profile**.

Next, I'm assuming you have a few friends and family. *If not, find some.* Send them "friend requests," and vice-versa. Next, post some photos of your family, your dog, your trip to Las Vegas or whatever to your "timeline," and when you login to Facebook on your desktop or your phone, look at your "news feed." Your news feed will show you the posts of the friends and family with whom you are connected: when they post to their "timeline," it will show in your "newsfeed" (with some caveats about *Edgerank*, more about this later). Similarly, when you post to your timeline, those posts will show on the news feed of your friends when / if they log into Facebook whether on their computers or their phones. Here it is:

Johnnie and I are **friends** on Facebook.

Johnnie **posts** pictures of his Lab puppy on his Facebook **timeline**.

I see those pictures when I log in on my Facebook **newsfeed**.

Essentially Facebook is a **huge interactive scrapbook**: you post photos and writings to your timeline, and your friends and family see them in their news feed, where they can like, comment, or share them. And vice-versa: your friends post to their timeline, and you see it in your news feed.

FACEBOOK IS A SOCIAL SCRAPBOOK

Facebook is also like a big family and friends party: 24/7. People post messages about their lives and families, social events, causes they like/dislike, etc. Pay attention to what people are sharing on Facebook. Generally, you'll see it falls into the themes of fun, family, friends, and photos:

- **Photos.** Photos dominate Facebook! Photos of friends at the beach, at Disneyland, graduating from High School, new babies. People are constantly posting photos with short commentaries, generally about friends, family, and fun.
- **Friends, Family, Fun.** Whether shared in photo format, as an image, or as plain text, Facebook is a place where people share stuff about their friends and family.
- **Games, Social Contests, Groups** For some people, Facebook is a place for social games. There are also groups on Facebook which allow people to collaborate and communicate, as for example a "group" of people taking a High School class in US History.

- **Social Causes and Endorsements.** People often "endorse" causes they care about (e.g., Breast Cancer awareness, Gay & Lesbian issues, Save the Whales) and share "outrage" about issues that they disagree with.

So, third, using your own personal Facebook account, spend some quality time (ideally with your marketing team), just bopping around Facebook, observing what people are "doing" at this party. The marketing goal is to understand the vibe, the culture, of Facebook so that your company's marketing message will blend in.

You're also looking to see if your customers (or competitors) are on Facebook, and reverse engineer what they are doing, and why.

Facebook and Fake

Notice, also, that Facebook is also about "fake." By "fake," I mean that people generally do not share embarrassing news on Facebook. People are very likely to share photos of their family trip to Disneyland, their new Labrador puppy, or their endorsement of the San Francisco Red Cross. If they climb Mount Everest, you can be sure they'll take a selfie at the summit and post it to Facebook. They are not likely, however, to share news about their family struggles, their pending divorce, or their shameful addiction to candy corn and weight problems. In general, people put their best foot forward on Facebook: it's a social scrapbook in many ways about how life "should" be, rather than how life "is."

Fourth, as you explore Facebook, try to conceptualize its culture. Each social medium is different, and you'll quickly realize that if LinkedIn is a serious platform for job searches and business-to-business information, Facebook is a fun platform for sharing photos with friends and family.

Once you grasp that Facebook is friends, family, fun, photos, and fake... you'll be better positioned to brainstorm how to take your company or brand and make the message fit the medium. Because Facebook is about fun, it's a natural place for fun consumer brands like Whole Foods, REI, and Disney Cruises. It's a great place to share recipe ideas. It's a great place to share "how to" videos on how to pitch a tent, or enjoy a cruise with your kids. It's not such a great place for posts on taxes, divorce issues, how to buy an industrial fan for your pig farm and the like. Some companies will blend easily into the vibe of Facebook, while others will blend only with some brainstorming about how to be "fun" even if the product or service isn't that fun (dentistry? plastic surgery? insurance?). And some products or services just do not work on Facebook.

As you explore Facebook, pay attention to its culture and ask yourself the question (again and again), "Do my customers 'hang out' on Facebook?" If so, it will be a high priority social medium for you. If not, not. There is no necessity to be on Facebook (or Twitter, or Instagram, or LinkedIn), if your customers are not there!

>> Make an Inventory of Likes & Dislikes on Facebook

Before you dive into the technical details of Facebook, it's incredibly important to a) understand the culture of the social medium you are considering, and b) inventory what you like, and dislike, about other brands already on it. Imitation is the highest form of flattery: identifying successful brands and reverse engineering their marketing strategy is the easiest way to succeed on Facebook.

So, now we are going to shift gears from **profiles** (individuals) to **Pages** (companies). You'll want to identify companies that are on Facebook, and reverse engineer their marketing strategy.

How do you find companies to "like" on Facebook?

Answer: By understanding how to be a power Facebook searcher.

Ways to Search Facebook

First identify the keyword themes that matter to you and your potential customers. For example, if you are a maker of organic baby food, you would use the key phrases "organic food" and "baby food" to identify companies that are already on Facebook. As you find them, you'll be making an inventory of what you like / dislike about their Facebook marketing in terms of their cover photo, profile picture, tabs, and their posting strategy above all else. Remember: if you're going to throw a party, you'll inventory the party theme, decorations, invitations, and all the things you like / dislike to make an inventory for your own party planning.

Once you know the keywords, (for example, "organic food"), here are the two best ways to find commercial Pages to inventory for your Facebook marketing plan:

> **Method #1 On Facebook**, type into the search box "organic food." Next at the bottom click on where it says "See more." Next at the top tab click on "Pages." It's not the most elegant search engine (it's Facebook, and not Google). But in this way you can find Pages to browse in your industry. Here are screenshots:

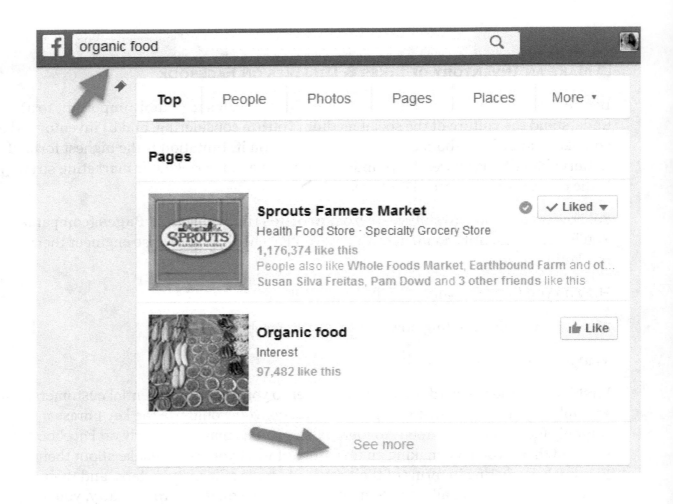

And then, after you click on "See more" -

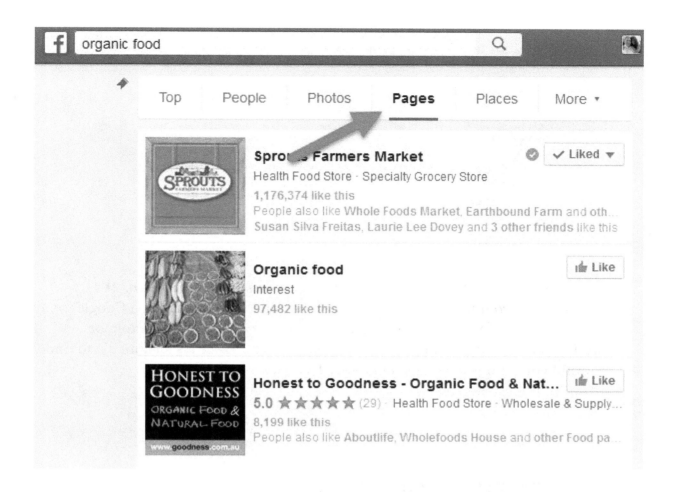

Then you'll see a list of relevant commercial Pages. You can click on each one, and begin your inventory of likes / dislikes.

Method #2 on Google. Go to Google (https://www.google.com/). Type into the Google search engine *site:facebook.com "organic food"*. Google will then return to you a list of commercial Pages on Facebook with that term in it. To see this in action, go to http://jmlinks.com/2i.

Here's a screenshot:

It's very important that there be no space between *site* and *the colon*. It's
site:facebook.com not *site: facebook.com*. You can use this tactic on Google for any
social media; as for example, *site:yelp.com massage therapists boston*, or
site:twitter.com industrial fans. It's a great way to browse a social media to find
relevant companies to reverse engineer. To see this in action, go to
http://jmlinks.com/2i.

IDENTIFY COMPANIES WHO DO FACEBOOK MARKETING WELL,

AND REVERSE ENGINEER THEM

Don't be afraid to "like" companies via Facebook (even your competitors). In fact, I
strongly encourage it: by "liking" companies you actually "like," you'll experience them
marketing to you, and you can then reverse engineer this for your own company. Once
you've set up a Page for your company, you can even click on the Insights tab, and
identify companies you want to follow by clicking on "Pages to watch."

Once you "like" a company, its posts will show up in your news feed (depending on
Edgerank). Facebook gives priority to posts by humans (friends and family), so to find
posts from brands you have liked, scan the left column of Facebook and look for a link to

what is called "Pages Feed." Click on that, and you'll see posts from companies that you have liked. Here's a screenshot:

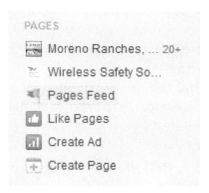

If you are logged into Facebook, you can also click on this link: https://www.facebook.com/pages/feed.

For your first TODO, download the **Facebook Research Worksheet**. For the worksheet, go to https://www.jm-seo.org/workbooks (click on Facebook, enter the code 'facebook2016' to register if you have not already done so), and click on the link to the "Facebook Research Worksheet." You'll answer questions as to whether your potential customers are on Facebook, identify brands to follow, and inventory what you like and dislike about their Facebook set up and marketing strategy.

» UNDERSTAND THE IMPORTANCE OF LIKE AND EDGERANK

To market successfully on Facebook, you need a detailed understanding of its **structure** and how it works. Most importantly, you need to understand the difference between a profile and a Page, and what "like" means vis-a-vis a Page and/or a Post, as well as comment and share.

For your inventory, you'll need to know some vocabulary about what is what on Facebook. Here's a synopsis:

- **People have "profiles."** This is Jason McDonald, a real person, for example. I have a *profile* (not a *Page*) on Facebook.
- **When two people "friend" each other by exchanging a "friend request," Facebook puts them in a "like" relationship.** If I "friend" my

friend, Tom Jones, and he accepts this request, then he and I are connected via Facebook.

- **When two profiles are connected, if person A posts to his timeline, person B will see that post on his news feed** (with the *Edgerank* caveat that the news feed can be very busy, and Facebook prioritizes the posts of friends with whom you interact over those whom you ignore).
  - o **People interact with a post** by "liking" the post, "commenting" on the post, and/or "sharing" the post, thereby essentially re-posting it to their own timeline so that their own friends can see / interact with the post. In the background Facebook ***Edgerank*** keeps track of which Pages and which posts are the most interactive, and favors them in the newsfeed across the social network.
- **Companies have Pages, not profiles.** A *profile* (person) creates a *Page* (company) and then manages it as an Admin. A Facebook Page can (and should) have more than one Admin. The *Page* for the JM Internet Group (https://www.facebook.com/jm.internet) is managed by me (a *profile*) for example.
  - o Pages can NOT exist without sponsorship by at least one profile!
  - o Any Admin can delete / change / post to a Page!
  - o Therefore, have at least two reliable, trustworthy Page Admins at all times.
  - o Before you fire someone, REMOVE him or her as a Page Admin!
- **When a person ("profile") "likes" a business "Page" that creates a Facebook relationship between the "profile" and the "Page."** When I "like" Safeway (https://www.facebook.com/Safeway), that means that when Safeway posts to its timeline, it might show on my news feed. By "liking" Safeway, I have given it permission to talk to me via Facebook.
  - o **People interact with a post** by a Page by "liking" the post, "commenting" on the post, and/or "sharing" the post, thereby essentially re-posting it to their own timeline so that their own friends can see / interact with the post. In the background Facebook ***Edgerank*** keeps track of which Pages and which posts are the most interactive, and favors them in the newsfeed across the social network.

To read the Facebook help files on setting up a business Page, go to http://www.jmlinks.com/1c. Note that you can technically create not just "Pages" for local businesses or places, companies, organizations, or institutions, and brands or products. You can create "public figure Pages" for artists, bands, or public figures (think CEO of your company, a la Martha Stewart), or even Pages for causes or communities. For most companies, you'll choose either the local business option, the company option, or the brand / product option. To see the options, go to https://www.facebook.com/pages/create/.

It Gets Complicated

Here's where it gets complicated. Remember our Social Media Marketing goals? Among them: staying top of mind, and encouraging social sharing? *Edgerank*, which is part of the Facebook algorithm, intervenes at this point. When a Page posts to its timeline, that post will show up on the news feed of "profiles" (people) who have liked it based on several factors:

- The individual ("profile") must have "liked" the Page in advance.
- If the individual previously "liked" the Page, and generally "liked" posts by the Page and/or commented on them and/or shared them, then the *Edgerank* of that Page is improved. The higher the *Edgerank* (based on more interaction between me and that Page), the more likely it is that the post by the Page will show in my timeline.
- A realtime analysis of the post: the faster and wider a post gets interactivity (likes, comments, and shares), the larger its Edgerank and it, therefore, gets even more publicity.

In essence, Facebook monitors whether you interact with the posts of a Page: the more you interact with those posts, the higher the Edgerank of that Page, and the more likely you are to continue to see posts by the Page in your news feed.

To use an example, let's look at the Mayo Clinic and me on Facebook.

1. I "like" the Mayo Clinic Page on Facebook (https://www.facebook.com/MayoClinic), giving it permission to talk to me via Facebook.
2. The Mayo Clinic posts images, photos, blog post summaries, etc., to its Facebook Page timeline, such as tips on how to live healthy, information on diseases, and even information on how to keep your pets healthy.
3. I "like" these posts, I "comment" on these posts (*"Oh, yes, I am going to eat more kale!"*), and even better I "share" these posts on my own timeline by clicking the share button.

Here's a screenshot of a post by the Mayo Clinic appearing on my Facebook news feed. I have highlighted in yellow the like / comment / share buttons at the bottom:

Mayo Clinic
4 hrs ·

"The presence of Mayo Clinic has turned Rochester, Minnesota into a thriving destination for reluctant tourists from every state and 140 countries. Roughly 40 percent of the 400,000 patients seen at Mayo's main campus here each year come from outside a 500-mile radius, including more than 8,500 international patients. They are traveling not to tropical beaches or ski slopes but to doctors, nurses, and expertise."
http://bit.ly/1g2SlI3

Rochester thrives as destination medical center for reluctant tourists flocking to Mayo Clinic

Rochester, Minn., with its population of just over 100,000 and its iconic water tower painted like an oversized ear of corn, may not be a place many would...

WWW.BOSTONG...COM

Like · Comment · Share · 2,662 157 441

By "liking," "commenting," or "sharing" this post, I am telling Facebook I am engaged with the Mayo Clinic Page. The more I do this, the more I will see its posts in my news feed.

Now, flip this around as marketers, our goals become:

- To increase our *Edgerank* (and the probability that people will see our posts in their newsfeed), we MUST get more likes, comments, and shares of our posts.
- To increase our *Edgerank*, we must get **interactivity**!

Encouraging interactivity is the name of the game when it comes to Facebook marketing. **Posting strategy** is all about what you post, and using those posts to drive up interactivity, and improve your Edgerank.

Next up, what kind of posts do people generally interact with? As marketers, we want to reverse engineer what gets interactivity on Facebook. For the most part: emotion, emotion, emotion. Posts that create emotional engagement tend to get the most interaction, for example:

- **Sentimental Posts**. Posts of kittens and puppies, posts of kids, posts of moms and dads, posts of moms and dads holding kittens and puppies. Posts about the 4th of July, posts about how much you love a cause... Brands on Facebook often post "sentimentality bait": posts that people click "like" on to indicate that they "agree" with the cause. So every mother's day, you can see brands posting pictures of mothers and their kids, and people clicking "like" on these posts because the "like" their mothers... which is increasing the Edgerank of these Pages.
- **Utility**. Posts that explain "how to do" stuff, especially things that are counterintuitive.
- **Counterintuitive**. Posts that take things you "think" you know, and explain that they don't really work like you think they do. Especially common are things that people "think" are safe, but in fact are dangerous such as rawhide dog chews (who knew that they were dangerous?).
- **Funny**. Humor is big on Facebook. Posting jokes, funny quotes, videos, images (memes), etc. Things that make people laugh, get them to click like, comment, or share. Queue the funny babies, babies with dogs, and of course cat videos.
- **Surveys, Polls, Contests**. Asking your audience a question, and getting them to use the comments as a way to interact with that. Take this quiz and learn which Star Trek character best describes your love life.
- **Quotes**. Sentimental, humorous, make-you-think quotes.
- **Outrage**. Things that make people mad: mad enough to comment, "like" in the sense of opposing the thing that outrages them, and even share. Outrage is very big on Facebook, and brands (rather cynically) leverage this outrage to increase their Edgerank. Click "like" if you think dolphins shouldn't die in Tuna nets, animals shouldn't be abused, etc., for example.

Thus in terms of **posting strategy**, brands will post items that are specifically engineered to increase engagement and thereby increase their *Edgerank*. Look back at the brands you like, and begin to notice how they are using the strategies above to increase interaction.

EDGERANK REWARDS YOU FOR INTERACTIVE POSTS

Here are some brands that I admire in terms of their Facebook marketing, all of which build Edgerank by sharing interactive content on a regular basis:

Navy Federal Credit Union (https://www.facebook.com/NavyFederal) – if you monitor its Page, you'll see a steady dose of sentimentality, especially pictures of military men with babies (a double whammy: *yes, I support our troops, and, yes, I like babies*!).

REI (https://www.facebook.com/REI**).** REI is an outdoor, sports retailer and uses Facebook to share "how to" information about hiking, campaign, and other outdoor sports, promote its products, and build a community around people who like the outdoors (and love its products).

The White House (https://www.facebook.com/WhiteHouse) – like him, hate him, I don't care, Barack Obama is our first "social media" president, and you can learn a ton from watching how his White House uses Facebook to spread its message, grow its political base, and just generally be cool.

Taco Bell (https://www.facebook.com/tacobell) – the edgy, youth brand is a master at building awareness, creating the "fourth meal" (just what obese America needed), and making factory food fun.

Metamucil (https://www.facebook.com/MetaWellness1) – there, I admit it. I use Metamucil! Any brand that can take something so, private, and grow a Facebook page to 209, 000 fans, has got to be doing something right. "Reverse engineer" how a product you probably didn't think of as friends, family, and fun uses social media on a regular basis (pun intended).

The Super Dentists (https://www.facebook.com/TheSuperDentists) – similarly to Metamucil, this San Diego kids dentists takes something not-so-fun (dentistry) and effectively builds eWom, one-touch-to-many, and even social sharing via pictures, contests, sentimentality posts and the like.

Father Robert Barron (https://www.facebook.com/FrRobertBarron) – known as the Catholic social media superstar, Fr. Barron shares history and theological insights, and shows how something as ancient as Catholicism can leverage new media to grow its reach and build its brand.

Make a list of your own favorite brands, "like" them on Facebook, and constantly "reverse engineer" their marketing strategy. Imitation, after all, is the highest form of flattery.

Posting Rhythm

Now the point of all this, as marketers, isn't that we really love babies and military personnel (although we probably do). It's to

- Increase our *Edgerank* to increase the probability that our Facebook fans will see our posts.
- Use our built-up *Edgerank* to propel posts that market our products or services into the news feeds of our fans, for free.

This gets to **posting rhythm**. Smart marketers will post ten, twenty "fun, fun, fun" posts to drive UP their Edgerank, and then one "buy, buy, buy my stuff" post that has a good chance of showing in the newsfeed. So the posting rhythm can be: *fun, fun, fun, fun, fun, fun, buy my stuff, fun, fun, fun, fun, fun, fun.* Even better, business Pages on Facebook will post items that their fans are likely to share with their own friends.

The reason for this is that the *Edgerank* of people is much, much higher than the *Edgerank* of company Pages. So, to the extent that you can create a post that will be shared on Facebook, you can get your fans to market your company's products.

Let me repeat that:

The Edgerank of people is much higher than the Edgerank of company Pages. **So getting your customers to share your posts is a fundamental component of an effective Facebook marketing strategy.**

To find out what's being shared in your industry, I recommend using Buzzsumo (http://www.buzzsumo.com/). Enter a keyword phrase, and Buzzsumo will tell you the highest shared content on Facebook in the past year, month, week or even day.

For example, here's a post of a military dad with a baby by Navy Federal Credit Union that got 854 "likes," 15 "comments," and 43 "shares":

Navy Federal Credit Union with Timothy Jump and 2 others

June 21 at 5:09am · 🌐

Tag your hero to wish him a Happy Father's Day!

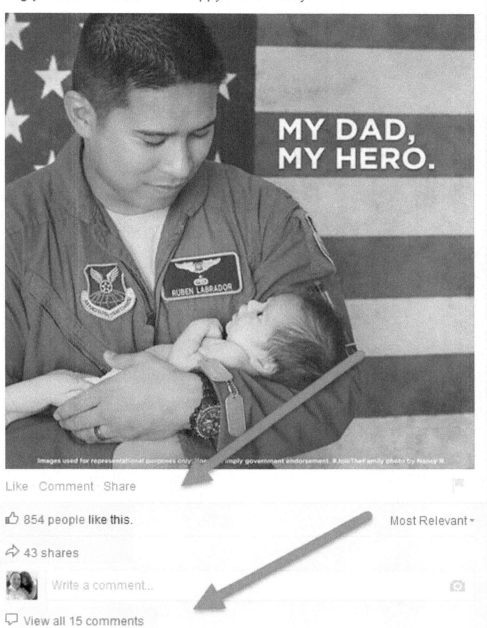

MY DAD,
MY HERO.

Images used for representational purposes only, does not imply government endorsement. #JoinTheFamily photo by Nancy N.

Like · Comment · Share

👍 854 people like this.

↪ 43 shares

Most Relevant ▾

Write a comment...

💬 View all 15 comments

And here's a shameless "buy our stuff" post. Notice how few likes, comments, and shares it garnered:

If you reverse engineer what Navy Federal Credit Union is doing on Facebook, it's posting items to drive up interactivity (fun stuff), and then occasionally posting items that are aimed to sell its products or services (serious stuff). So the posting rhythm is:

fun, fun, fun, fun, fun, fun, fun, fun, fun, **buy our stuff***, fun, fun, fun, fun, fun, fun, fun,* **buy our stuff***, fun, fun, fun, etc.*

There are two factors at work here:

Edgerank: improving the *Edgerank* of posts by a Page, improves the *Edgerank* of its posts. (Note: this is also a reason to pay attention to the time of day, because *Edgerank* is determined "on the fly," and if a post does well "out of the gate," it will tend to do better over time).

Social Sharing. Getting the fans of a Page to share the posts to their own friends and family.

Generally speaking, posts that are highly interactive get boosts on both measures. As you reverse engineer the posting strategy of competitors and/or brands you admire on Facebook, notice how they try to spur either one or both of the above.

⏩ SET UP AND OPTIMIZE YOUR FACEBOOK PAGE

Now that you've got the basics of Facebook down, it's time to set up or optimize your Page. A good way to do this is to compare / contrast Pages that you like and use your inventory list to identify ToDos. So, comparing Taco Bell (https://www.facebook.com/tacobell) the White House (https://www.facebook.com/WhiteHouse), and The Super Dentists (https://www.facebook.com/TheSuperDentists), let's go down item by item your set up todos.

Login to your Facebook Page, and then use the top menu.

- **Page Admins**. Your Page needs at least one Admin (you), but I recommend more than one. Realize that anyone who is an Admin can post to the Page, and also delete any other Admins. Your Admins should be reliable, and if you ever part ways (e.g., fire them), be sure to remove them as an Admin. *Located under Settings > Page Roles*
- **General Settings** (*Located under Settings > General*)
  - **Visitor Posts**. This setting allows users to post to the Page as well as add photos or videos. Note that Taco Bell has this "on" (anyone can post to the Page) vs. the White House, which has this "off." If you trust your fans, turn it on. If you're concerned about spam and controversy, turn it off.
  - **Tagging Ability**. Similar to the above, allows users to "tag" others in photos.
  - **Page Moderation and Profanity Filter**. You can turn on filters that block naughty words like the "f" word, and/or enter specific words. If a

user attempts to post or comment using these words, they will be blocked from your Page.

  - ○ **Other items**. Scroll through the list, and you can find other miscellaneous items such as banned users, post attribution, and notifications. For most of these, the default settings are fine.
- **About Your Page**. *Located under Settings > General > Page Info or click on the About Tab*. Fill out this information in detail. Note that if you are a "local Page" and you have a physical "address," this will turn on the **Review tab** and allow users to review your Page.

Among important Page set up issues are:

- **Ability to Post to the Page**. If you are confident that your user community will help your brand, I recommend turning this "on," as this allows users to post information to your Page, and thereby encourages social sharing and spread. If you are worried about hostile or naughty users, turn this off. Taco Bell has this on; the White House has this off. You can see this by looking at their Facebook Pages, and notice that on Taco Bell's it shows you a Post box and says "write something."
- **Local Business Address**. If you enter a physical address and your Page type is local business, then the **review tab** will be enabled. This allows users to review your Page and/or business. Turn it "on," if you think reviews will help you. If mobile users are important, this will also enable them to "**check in**" when they are at your business – and remember, when they "check in," Facebook will alert their friends (social sharing). (The Super Dentists (https://www.facebook.com/TheSuperDentists) has this on).
- **Call to Action Button**. This allows you to promote an action such as sign up for our newsletter, watch a video, etc. For an explanation, visit http://jmlinks.com/1d. Taco Bell has this set up for "use app." Available actions are: Book Now, Contact Us, Use App, Play Game, Shop Now, Sign Up, or Watch Video.

Set up Your Cover Photo and Profile Picture

Now that you've completed the basic structural set up for your Page, it's time to think about the graphic elements: the **cover photo** and the **profile picture**. The cover photo, of course, is the long horizontal photo that visitors see when they visit your Page. The profile picture is the square box that identifies your Page, both when they visit your Page and as a small icon when you post something that shows in their news feed. If you pay attention to companies like Taco Bell, the White House, Navy Federal Credit Union and the like, you'll see that they systematically rotate their cover photos. When a new cover photo is uploaded, that creates a post and an opportunity to alert your fans Any change in the cover photo in particular "broadcasts" that change to people who like the Page.

For the technical specifications on changing your cover photo and/or profile picture, visit http://jmlinks.com/1e. The cover photo in particular is an opportunity for fun, high-quality photos and for seasonal rotations. Follow a vendor like REI (https://www.facebook.com/REI), and you'll see not only seasonal rotation but also thematic unity among their cover photos on Twitter (https://twitter.com/rei), Facebook, Instagram (https://instagram.com/rei/), etc.

For your second TODO, download the **Facebook Setup Worksheet**. For the worksheet, go to https://www.jm-seo.org/workbooks (click on Facebook, enter the code 'facebook2016' to register if you have not already done so), and click on the link to the "Facebook Setup Worksheet." You'll answer and outline the basic setup issues for your Facebook Page.

≫ BRAINSTORM AND EXECUTE A POSTING STRATEGY

Content is king, and queen, and jack. Now that you've set up your Facebook Page, you need to think about posting. Turn back to your Content Marketing plan, and remember you'll need both other people's content and your own content to post:

- **Photographs and Images**. Facebook is very visual, and you'll need to systematically identify photographs and images that fit with your brand message and ideally encourage likes, comments, and shares.
- **Blog Posts Summaries**. To the extent that you have an active blog and are posting items that fit with friends, family, and fun, post headlines, short summaries and links to your blog.
  - Note that the first or "featured" image will become the shareable image, and that the META DESCRIPTION will become the default description when sharing. Choose striking, fun images for your blog posts!
- **Quotes**. People love quotes, and taking memorable quotes and pasting them on graphics is a win/win.
- **Infographics and Instructographics**. Factoids, how to articles, especially ones that are fun, are excellent for Facebook.
- **Quizzes, Surveys, and Response-provoking posts**. Ask a question, and get an answer or more. Great for encouraging interactivity.

Turn to the content marketing section of the *Social Media Toolbook* for a list of tools that will help you find other people's content and create your own. I recommend Hootsuite (https://www.hootsuite.com/) to manage all your social postings across platforms.

For your third Todo, download the **Facebook Posting Worksheet**. For the worksheet, go to https://www.jm-seo.org/workbooks (click on Facebook, enter the code 'facebook2016' to register if you have not already done so), and click on the link to the "Facebook Posting Worksheet." You'll systematically built out a posting strategy based on other people's content and your own content.

Once you get this done, it's time to post. Remember that Facebook marketing requires a commitment of time and resources. You can even create an editorial calendar and assigned Todos for your team so that every week you are posting to Facebook on a regular basis.

How frequently should you post?

Now that the Facebook news feed is very crowded, you can safely post quite frequently: even several times a day. But this differs with your audience, so pay attention using the Insights tab as to what posts get the best response, and whether the time of day matters. Pay attention as well to your Page likes and unlikes, to see if your posts are delighting or annoying your followers.

Experiment and measure, and you'll figure out a posting rhythm that works for you.

POST 80% OR MORE ABOUT "FUN," AND 20% OR LESS ABOUT "BUY MY STUFF."

Don't forget that most of your posts (80% or more) should be about friends, family, and fun, and only a few (20% or less) should be direct pitches to buy your stuff. If you oversell your stuff, your *Edgerank* will suffer and your fans will unlike your Page. Finally, you can "pin" a post to the top of your Page, so that it is the first post people will see. Just click on the down chevron on the top right corner of Facebook, and select the downward chevron to "pin" the post to the top.

>> PROMOTE YOUR FACEBOOK PAGE AND POSTS

Once you've set up your Page, and begun to populate it with posts on a regular basis, you've essential "set up" the party. Now it's time to send out the invitations. In and of itself, a Facebook Page will not be self-promoting!

Remember: social media is a party. You must have yummy yummy food and entertainment for people to show up, and stick around. So as you promote your Facebook Page, always keep front and center "what's in it for them" – what will they get by "liking" your Facebook page, and checking it out on a regular basis?

Assuming your Page has lots of yummy yummy content, here are some common ways to promote your Page:

- **Real World to Social.** Don't forget the real world! If you are a museum store, for example, be sure that the cashiers recommend to people that they "like" your Facebook Page? *Why? Because they'll get insider tips, fun do-it-yourself posts, announcements on upcoming museum and museum store events, etc.*
- **Cross-Promotion**. Link your website to your Facebook Page, your blog posts to your Facebook Page, your Twitter to your Facebook Page, etc. Notice how big brands like REI do this: one digital property promotes another digital property.
- **Email**. Email your customer list and ask them to "like" your Page. Again, you must have a reason why they'll like it: what's in it for them? Have a contest, give away something for free, or otherwise motivate them to click from the email to your Page, and then "like" the Page.
- **Facebook Internal**. Interact with other Pages, share their content, comment on timely topics using #hashtags, and reach out to complementary Pages to work with you on co-promotion. Internal promotion is not particularly strong on Facebook, but it should still be in the mix.
- **Use Facebook Plugins**. Facebook has numerous plugins that allow you to "embed" your Facebook Page on your website, and thereby nurture cross promotion. To learn more about plugins, visit https://developers.facebook.com/docs/plugins. If you are using WordPress, you can use the official Facebook plugin at https://wordpress.org/plugins/facebook/. In this way, your blog can promote your Facebook Page, and your Facebook Page can promote your blog. Similarly, your YouTube videos can promote your Facebook Page, and your Facebook Page can promote your YouTube Videos.

- **Leverage your Fans**. People who like your Page are your best promoters. When they first like your Page, when they comment on a post, when they "check in" to your local business on Facebook, and especially when they share your posts, their friends see this. Remember, it's *social* (!) media, and encouraging your customers to share your content is the name of the game. You want to leverage your fans as much as possible to share your content.

GET YOUR FANS TO SHARE YOUR POSTS ON FACEBOOK

Advertise. Advertising is increasingly important to success on Facebook. Just a few years back, Pages could really grow organically and be seen organically in the news feed. With the news feed increasingly crowded, Facebook has clearly prioritized content from real people over content from brands, and all but hidden the brand Pages. In many ways, Facebook has become pay to play. Here are ways you can promote your Page and posts through advertising.

> **Promote Your Page**. When you log in as a Page administrator, you'll see a blue button called "promote your Page." Click on that, and then follow the instructions to demographically target potential customers. Facebook will then suggest your Page to people, as a Page to "like." You can even specifically target certain demographic groups (such as your competitor's customers).

> **Boost your Posts**. When you make a post to Facebook, a blue boost button will appear on the bottom. If you click boost, you can demographically target an audience as well as "boost" your Post to people who already like your Page.

The great thing about Facebook advertising is that it is demographically targeted. You can even target a competitor's Facebook audience to grow your own Page. *(Note: this is a growing criticism of Facebook by companies: Facebook "sells" your user community to the highest bidder, so you build up your audience and then they sell it to your competition).*

To learn more about Facebook advertising, visit https://www.facebook.com/advertising.

≫ MEASURE YOUR RESULTS

Facebook marketing offers pretty good metrics. Inside of Facebook, click on the **Insights** tab at the top of your Facebook Page (when you're logged in, of course). Here you'll find an overview to your Facebook activity, and a post-by-post breakdown of the reach of a post and the engagement. A graph will tell you when your fans are most engaged. You can select "Pages to watch," and keep an eye on your competitors – even down to which posts of theirs were the most interactive.

For any of your posts, click on the post, and a popup window will give you drill-down information. Remember: you are trying to improve *Edgerank*, so pay attention to the positive and negative interactivity. Here's a screenshot of a post of "other people's content" to the JM Internet Group Facebook Page:

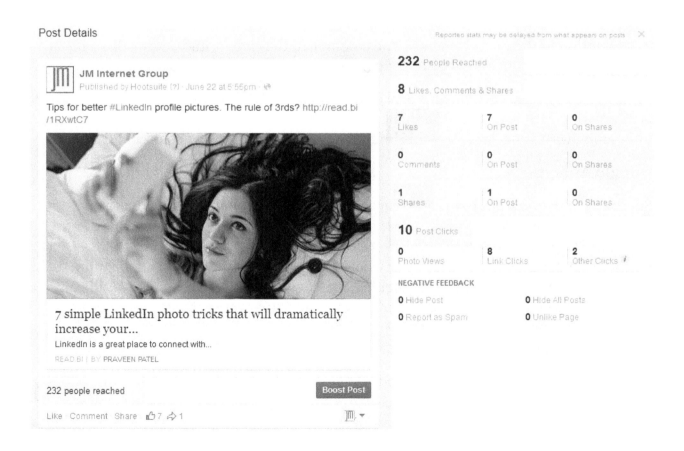

And here's a screenshot of a post of our own content that was boosted for $200.00

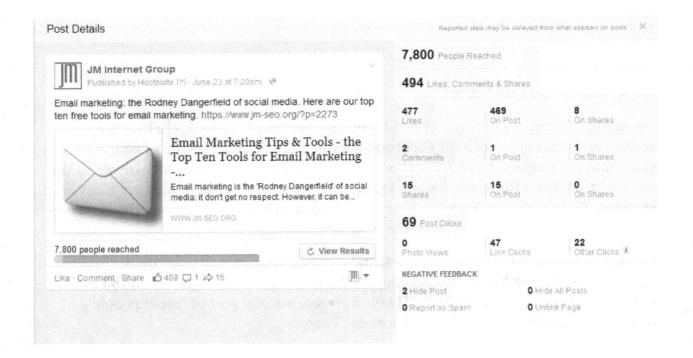

Pay attention to the reach, the likes, the comments, the shares, and clicks: all of this is influencing *Edgerank* and you are trying to propel that as high as possible.

Back to the top tabs, you can also drill down into people, to see the demographics of who is interacting with your Page. All in all, Facebook provides excellent insights into who is interacting with your Page. Use this information to make your Page better and better!

Google Analytics

For many of us, we want to drive traffic from Facebook to our website, even to our ecommerce store or to download a free eBook or software package to get a sales lead. Sign up for Google Analytics (https://www.google.com/analytics) and install the required tracking code. Inside of your Google Analytics account on the left column, drill down by clicking on Acquisition > Social > Overview. Then on the right hand side of the screen you'll see a list of Social Networks. Find Facebook on that list, and click on that. Google Analytics will tell you what URLs people clicked to from Facebook to your Website, giving you insights into what types of web content people find attractive.

You can also create a custom Advanced Segment to look at only Facebook traffic and its behavior. For information on how to create custom Advanced Segments in Google Analytics, go to http://jmlinks.com/1f. For the Google help files on Advanced Segments go to http://jmlinks.com/1g.

In sum, inside of Facebook you can see how people interact with your Page and posts. Inside of Google Analytics, you can see where they land on your website and what they do after they arrive.

» DELIVERABLE: A FACEBOOK MARKETING PLAN

Now that we've come to the end our chapter on Facebook, your DELIVERABLE has arrived. For the worksheet, go to https://www.jm-seo.org/workbooks (click on Facebook, enter the code 'facebook2016' to register if you have not already done so), and click on the link to the "Facebook Marketing Plan." By filling out this plan, you and your team will establish a vision of what you want to achieve via Facebook.

» TOP TEN FACEBOOK MARKETING TOOLS AND RESOURCES

Here are the top ten tools and resources to help you with Facebook marketing. For an up-to-date list, go to https://www.jm-seo.org/workbooks (click on Facebook, enter the code 'facebook2016' to register if you have not already done so), and click on the link to the *Social Media Toolbook* link, and drill down to the Facebook chapter.

FACEBOOK SOCIAL PLUGINS (LIKE BOXES AND BUTTONS) -
http://developers.facebook.com/docs/plugins

> Make it easy for your Facebook fans and fans-to-be to 'like' your company and Facebook Pages you create. The best Facebook resource for all plugins to integrate Facebook with your website, including the Like, Share & Send Button, Comments, Follow Button and others.
>
> **Rating:** 5 Stars | **Category:** tool

FACEBOOK HELP CENTER - http://facebook.com/help

> The 'missing' help Pages on Facebook. Useful for learning everything on the king of social media. Links on advertising, business accounts, connect, Facebook places and more.
>
> **Rating:** 5 Stars | **Category:** overview

FACEBOOK AUDIENCE INSIGHTS - https://facebook.com/ads/audience_insights

Facebook Audience Insights is a tool available within Facebook Ads Manager. It allows users to delve into Facebook user data to make better Ads purchasing decisions, but you don't have to purchase Facebook Ads to use the tool, or to benefit from the insights it can provide. Spend some time to learn more about your audience (vs all Facebook users), their demographics, interests, behavior so you can create better content, craft better messages, and ultimately engage them more effectively.

Rating: 5 Stars | **Category:** tool

FACEBOOK LIKE BUTTON FOR WEB - https://developers.facebook.com/docs/plugins/like-button

The Facebook Like button lets a user share your content with friends on Facebook. When the user clicks the Like button on your site, a story appears in the user's friends' News Feeds with a link back to your website.

Rating: 5 Stars | **Category:** tool

SOCIALOOMPH - http://socialoomph.com

SocialOomph is a powerful free (and paid) suite of tools to manage and schedule your Twitter and Facebook posts. Imagine going to the beach, forgetting about the office, yet having 67 different Tweets auto-posted...that's what SocialOomph is about. Use technology to appear busy and Facebooking / Tweeting all the time.

Rating: 4 Stars | **Category:** tool

FACEBOOK ADVERTISING - http://facebook.com/advertising

Facebook advertising opportunities. Run text ads on Facebook by selecting the demographics of who you want to reach. Pay-per-click model.

Rating: 4 Stars | **Category:** overview

FACEBOOK FOR BUSINESS: MARKETING SOLUTIONS - http://facebook.com/marketing

Official Pages on Facebook-approved 'best practices' for marketing your company on Facebook.

Rating: 4 Stars | **Category:** overview

KEYHOLE - http://keyhole.co

This tool provides real-time social conversation tracking for Twitter, Facebook, and Instagram. Use this tool to measure conversations around your business, identify prospective clients and influencers talking about your services, and find relevant content. Enables tracking of hashtags, keywords, and URLs.

Rating: 4 Stars | **Category:** tool

LIKEALYZER - http://likealyzer.com

LikeAlyzer analyzes the Facebook Page you enter and provides a very simple, easy to read report even the most statistically averse will understand. Best of all, LikeAlyzer provides an overall score and recommendations on where/how to improve. Recommendations are customized and analysis is based on the metrics the company has found to be important: presence, dialogue, action and information.

Rating: 4 Stars | **Category:** tool

SHORTSTACK - http://shortstack.com

ShortStack is a nifty program to optimize your social media campaigns on platforms like Facebook, Twitter, Instagram and Pinterest. On Facebook, ShortStack provides polls and surveys, contents, and forms for newsletter signups, contact us, etc. and is free for Business Pages up to a certain number of Likes. No expiring trials. No credit card required.

Rating: 4 Stars | **Category:** service

FACEBOOK TOOLS

Facebook, like all social media, has a cornucopia of free resources and free tools to make your life easier. Below I produce my favorite tools and resources (in rank order). Remember that by registering your copy of the workbook, you can access the Social Media Toolbook, which has all the tools in convenient, clickable PDF format. To register, go to https://www.jm-seo.org/workbooks (click on Facebook, enter the code 'facebook2016' to register if you have not already done so), and click on the link to the *Social Media Toolbook*.

Here are free Facebook tools and resources, sorted with the best items first.

FACEBOOK SOCIAL PLUGINS (LIKE BOXES AND BUTTONS) -
http://developers.facebook.com/docs/plugins

> Make it easy for your Facebook fans and fans-to-be to 'like' your company and Facebook pages you create. The best Facebook resource for all plugins to integrate Facebook with your website, including the Like, Share & Send Button, Comments, Follow Button and others.
>
> **Rating:** 5 Stars | **Category:** tool

FACEBOOK HELP CENTER - http://facebook.com/help

> The 'missing' help pages on Facebook. Useful for learning everything on the king of social media. Links on advertising, business accounts, connect, Facebook places and more.
>
> **Rating:** 5 Stars | **Category:** overview

FACEBOOK AUDIENCE INSIGHTS - https://facebook.com/ads/audience_insights

Facebook Audience Insights is a tool available within Facebook Ads Manager. It allows users to delve into Facebook user data to make better Ads purchasing decisions, but you don't have to purchase Facebook Ads to use the tool, or to benefit from the insights it can provide. Spend some time to learn more about your audience (vs all Facebook users), their demographics, interests, behavior so you can create better content, craft better messages, and ultimately engage them more effectively.

Rating: 5 Stars | **Category:** tool

FACEBOOK LIKE BUTTON FOR WEB -
https://developers.facebook.com/docs/plugins/like-button

The Facebook Like button lets a user share your content with friends on Facebook. When the user clicks the Like button on your site, a story appears in the user's friends' News Feeds with a link back to your website.

Rating: 5 Stars | **Category:** tool

SOCIALOOMPH - http://socialoomph.com

SocialOomph is a powerful free (and paid) suite of tools to manage and schedule your Twitter and Facebook posts. Imagine going to the beach, forgetting about the office, yet having 67 different Tweets auto-posted...that's what SocialOomph is about. Use technology to appear busy and Facebooking / Tweeting all the time.

Rating: 4 Stars | **Category:** tool

FACEBOOK ADVERTISING - http://facebook.com/advertising

Facebook advertising opportunities. Run text ads on Facebook by selecting the demographics of who you want to reach. Pay-per-click model.

Rating: 4 Stars | **Category:** overview

FACEBOOK FOR BUSINESS: MARKETING SOLUTIONS - http://facebook.com/marketing

Official pages on Facebook-approved 'best practices' for marketing your company on Facebook.

Rating: 4 Stars | **Category:** overview

KEYHOLE - http://keyhole.co

This tool provides real-time social conversation tracking for Twitter, Facebook, and Instagram. Use this tool to measure conversations around your business, identify prospective clients and influencers talking about your services, and find relevant content. Enables tracking of hashtags, keywords, and URLs.

Rating: 4 Stars | **Category:** tool

LIKEALYZER - http://likealyzer.com

LikeAlyzer analyzes the Facebook Page you enter and provides a very simple, easy to read report even the most statistically averse will understand. Best of all, LikeAlyzer provides an overall score and recommendations on where/how to improve. Recommendations are customized and analysis is based on the metrics the company has found to be important: presence, dialogue, action and information.

Rating: 4 Stars | **Category:** tool

SHORTSTACK - http://shortstack.com

ShortStack is a nifty program to optimize your social media campaigns on platforms like Facebook, Twitter, Instagram and Pinterest. On Facebook, ShortStack provides polls and surveys, contents, and forms for newsletter signups, contact us, etc. and is free for Business Pages up to a certain number of Likes. No expiring trials. No credit card required.

Rating: 4 Stars | **Category:** service

SMALL BUSINESS GUIDE TO FACEBOOK - http://simplybusiness.co.uk/microsites/facebook-for-small-businesses

Interactive step-by-step flowchart to using Facebook for small business. Comprised of key questions and linked resources with more information. Chart is divided into different areas including goals and measurement, engagement, page management, Facebook ads, and advanced tips. Worth a look.

Rating: 4 Stars | **Category:** resource

FACEBOOK PAGE BASICS (FOR BUSINESS) -
https://www.facebook.com/business/learn/facebook-page-basics

Confused by Facebook for Business? Have no fear, Learn How, Facebook's online learning center for businesses, is here. This easy-to-use resource, complete with videos, images and step-by-step instructions, answers businesses' frequently asked questions, like how to create a Page, and how to create a Custom Audience. Learn How content is organized to be flexible: use it in-depth, or as a reference library as questions arise.

Rating: 4 Stars | **Category:** tutorial

IFTTT - https://ifttt.com

This app, If Then Then That, is a great tool for linking multiple social media accounts. It allows you to create 'recipes' that link your tools exactly the way you like them! For example: make a recipe that adds to a Google Apps spreadsheet every time a particular user uploads to Instagram - a great way to keep up with your competitors SMM strategies! With over 120 supported applications, the 'recipes' are endless, making this a good tool for your SMM strategies.

Rating: 4 Stars | **Category:** tool

FACEBOOK PAGES HELP CENTER - https://facebook.com/help/281592001947683

Here it is. The help center for Facebook 'pages', where businesses, organizations, and brands live. Use this handy dandy resource from Facebook to answer your most basic questions - such as how to set up a page for a business, how to administer your page (e.g., comments, kicking users off and all that fun stuff), as well as how to manage admins. It is the first 'goto' page for help with Facebook Pages for business.

Rating: 4 Stars | **Category:** resource

DEFINITIVE GUIDE TO FACEBOOK INSIGHTS FOR BUSINESS - http://hostopiablog.verticalresponse.com/blog/a-definitive-guide-to-using-facebook-insights-for-your-business/

Overwhelmed by Facebook Insights? Not sure where to begin? Refer to this handy guide to make sense of the trove of data Facebook makes available for both Pages and its users (Audience). This page is brief, but comprehensive, the perfect starting point for your foray into Facebook analytics.

Rating: 3 Stars | **Category:** overview

TABSITE - http://tabsite.com

Powerful Facebook Page tab builder with a wide array of apps including sweepstakes, contents, coupons, and more. Most features require paid plan though these apps are currently available free: Image App, E-mail Sign-up App, Timeline Contest App.

Rating: 3 Stars | **Category:** service

FACEBOOK PAGE RANKING - https://www.quintly.com/facebook-page-ranking/

This nifty tool helps you find the highest ranked pages in any one of dozens of Facebook categories and allows you to sort them by number of Likes, People Talking About This and net and percent change for these statistics over the last 30 days.

Rating: 3 Stars | **Category:** resource

FACEBOOK BOOST YOUR POSTS - https://facebook.com/help/547448218658012/

Not a free tool in any way shape or form, but still important. A boosted post is way to jump to the head of the Facebook line. Separate yourself from a little cash, and get Facebook to 'promote' your post to your fans a little longer, a little more prominently.

Rating: 3 Stars | **Category:** service

TWITTER TAB ON FACEBOOK - https://apps.facebook.com/twitter-tab-app

This slick little app allows you to easily add your Twitter feed to your Facebook page as a tab. You can also do this for Instagram and a Pinterest. It's very, very easy, and free!

Rating: 3 Stars | **Category:** service

FACEBOOK AWARDS - http://facebook-studio.com/awards/about

If need some creative inspiration for your Facebook business page, peruse the Facebook Awards. These awards, established by Facebook, celebrate the best creative work on the social network, as chosen by some of the top creatives in the industry. Not only do they recognize excellence in execution, they set the bar for creative growth and evolution on Facebook. Check them and see!

Rating: 3 Stars | **Category:** resource

WOOBOX - http://woobox.com

Create coupons, sweepstakes, photo contests, polls, and custom Facebook tabs to woo your fans. Simply, the most viral features anywhere for the best price. Facebook tabs for Twitter, Instagram, Pinterest, and Google+, it's all here.

Rating: 3 Stars | **Category:** vendor

TABFUSION - http://tabfusion.com

Tabs on Facebook allow you to present third party content such as videos. Tabfusion helps you do that - free for individuals, fee for companies.

Rating: 3 Stars | **Category:** service

FACEBOOK DEVELOPERS PAGE - http://developers.facebook.com

One of the great things about Facebook is the applications or apps available on the platform. This is the primary developer page, a gateway to finding apps especially for your blog or other resources.

Rating: 2 Stars | **Category:** resource

FANGAGER - http://fangager.com

Service providing Facebook fan analytics, management, and engagement tools. With it, you can not only identify top fans, but can create activities (e.g., posting, commenting, liking, tweeting) or contests with rewards (e.g., badges, virtual gifts, or real prizes) to boost fan interaction.

Rating: 2 Stars | **Category:** service

FANPAGE KARMA - http://fanpagekarma.com

Fanpage Karma is another Facebook Page analytics tool, providing all sorts of valuable information like growth, engagement, service and response time, and of course Karma (a weighted engagement value). Free plan provides reports for only one page, along with limited features.

Rating: 2 Stars | **Category:** tool

FACEBOOK GRID TOOL - https://facebook.com/ads/tools/text_overlay

If you're going to advertise on Facebook, the amount of text an image can have is limited to 20%. This tool will measure that for you, to ensure your image will be accepted by Facebook. Are these people control freaks or what?

Rating: 2 Stars | **Category:** tool

PAGEMODO - http://pagemodo.com

Pagemodo is an online tool which enables businesses and Facebook Page owners to design and build their own customized Facebook pages, including cover photos, contests, custom tabs, designing and scheduling posts, and Facebook Ads. Limited functionality available with free account, pay more for additional features.

Rating: 2 Stars | **Category:** tool

PINVOLVE - http://pinvolve.co

This tool automatically syncs your Facebook and Pinterest pages, allowing you to integrate your social media marketing strategies. Free for one Facebook page with limited pinning.

Rating: 2 Stars | **Category:** tool

FACEBOOK TIMELINE CONTEST - http://contest.agorapulse.com

Use this nifty free tool to create Facebook Timeline contests and engage fans. The tool lets you create three types of contests: sweepstakes, quizzes, and photo contests, and automatically selects the winner based on the type, thereby saving valuable time. Worth a look.

Rating: 2 Stars | **Category:** tool

PINTEREST FACEBOOK PAGE TAB - http://woobox.com/pinterest

This tool allows you to add a Pinterest tab to your Facebook page; another great way to integrate your social media marketing strategies! Get complete stats for page views, visits, and likes, segmented by fans and non-fans who view your Facebook page tab.

Rating: 2 Stars | **Category:** tool

FACEBOOK TIMELINE COVER BANNER - http://timelinecoverbanner.com

Use this online tool to design and create a custom Facebook cover image for your business or personal Facebook page.

Rating: 2 Stars | **Category:** tool

VIRALTAG - http://viraltag.com

Use this tool to plan and publish visual content to social media platforms. This is a great tool for managing multiple social media platforms at once and is is free for three social profiles.

Rating: 2 Stars | **Category:** tool

FACEBOOK FOR BUSINESS (ADS) - https://facebook.com/business

Facebook's resource hub for business has been refreshed, with a streamlined layout and new content that shows how businesses use Facebook to drive business goals. It includes customer success stories and the latest Facebook marketing news, though is quite salesy, so view with healthy dose of corporate skepticism.

Rating: 2 Stars | **Category:** resource